Dear Reader,

I would like to welcome you into this phase of your healing journey. After having dealt with molestation, abuse, bullying, mental illness, and so much more, the Lord God revealed to me that all of my pain and poor decision-making was a result of trauma caused by rejection and abandonment. By the time that I was 30yrs I had been sexually assaulted over 4 times by several different people. I had endured much pain through living a destructive lifestyle. This caused two in-patient stays & one intensive out patient at mental facilities. I suffered from severe PTSD. I was heavily medicated until God allowed people to come along side me in the journey. He healed my heart and I was able to come off of every single mood stabilizer.

I thank Jesus for saving me. I want to thank my loving husband for supporting me. My family, pastors, and mentors for pushing me to share my testimony. Finally, I want to thank YOU for trusting me enough to be a part of your healing.

As you go through this journey I pray that the Lord reveals to you, who He intends to be in your life. I pray that the Lord heals your heart from pain and trauma. I pray that He remove your dependency from anything other than Him. Finally, I pray that reading and working through this book will bless you as much as it has been a blessing to me. To God be all of the Glory.

I love you to life!

-N V

# TABLE OF CONTENTS

## 01 | Introduction

| | |
|---|---|
| Trauma Goggles | 03 |
| True Assessment | 05 |
| Healing at the Source | 08 |

## 02 | Childhood Trauma

| | |
|---|---|
| Arrested Development | 11 |
| The Child Within | 14 |
| Which Brother are You? | 16 |

## 03 | Deep Dive

| | |
|---|---|
| Your Good, His Glory | 18 |
| When There is No Justice | 21 |
| Hypothetical Loved One | 23 |
| Hypothetical Loved One II | 25 |

## 04 | Journal Entries

| | |
|---|---|
| Deception of Hyper Sexuality | 29 |
| Identity Crisis | 31 |
| The Emotion that's Not from God | 33 |
| They Did Not Earn You | 35 |

## 05 | Do the Work

| | |
|---|---|
| No More Self Harm | 38 |
| Abandonment of Loss | 40 |
| Healing your Support System | 42 |
| Procrastination Prison | 44 |
| Fearing What You Desire | 46 |

# Trauma Goggles

The way you see the world and your current experiences are shaped by a few key factors. Heritage culture, Household Culture and your Social culture. Now we are talking about developmental stages right now. However, these factors still apply as an adult.

So if you have experienced **rejection** and/or **abandonment** of any sort in any of these areas there is very likely that you also have a **trauma** associated with that experience. The significance of this is that your brain cannot compute **trauma** so it puts those situations in danger. Whenever the danger file is opened, your survival instincts will kick-in. These are your **fight**, **flight**, and **freeze** functions. This process is very challenging and requires most of your brain function. So what it does is shut off other non essential functions such as most cognition like decision making. Why is this relevant? I am so glad you asked! A trauma related to **rejection** and **abandonment** creates triggers in future relational interactions. And where there are unresolved triggers, there are poor choices.

Now that we have shed light on the medical side, let's take a moment to forgive ourselves for our poor choices during trigger points. Write your past self a letter and list the times that you made poor choices in school, work, church, with family, friends, sexually, and relationally. Describe how you were feeling in that moment of decision. You may find similarities in your mental state and even physical reactions. These are your rejection and abandonment goggles. They are warnings to let you know that you need to stop and retrain your brain to feel safe before you do something that will **hurt yourself**.

**"Peace has been stripped away, and I have forgotten what prosperity is. I cry out, "My splendor is gone! Everything I had hoped for from the Lord is lost!" The thought of my suffering and homelessness is bitter beyond words. I will never forget this awful time, as I grieve over my loss. Yet I still dare to hope when I remember this: The faithful love of the Lord never ends! His mercies never cease. Great is HIS faithfulness; HIS mercies begin afresh each morning. I say to myself, "The Lord is my inheritance; therefore, I will hope in HIM!"" LAM 3:24 NLT**

# Journal Moment

# True Assessment

I want to start today by saying that every adult has experienced **rejection** and **abandonment**. Not all **rejection** and **abandonment** is **traumatic** but all **mental** and **emotional trauma** is a result of **abandonment** or **rejection**. I'm going to list a number of ways that this can take place and I want you to check off the symptoms that have some relevance to you. Keep in mind that even if it did not directly happen to you, you still are a part of the experience and it still affected you.

Check ✓ ANY/ALL That Apply To You.

| | | |
|---|---|---|
| ☐ Low Self Esteem | ☐ Bitterness | ☐ Unforgiveness |
| ☐ Envy | ☐ Jealousy | ☐ Inferiority |
| ☐ Insecurity | ☐ Sadness | ☐ Inadequacy |
| ☐ Self Condemnation | ☐ Depression | ☐ Anxiety |
| ☐ Hopelessness | ☐ Selfishness | ☐ Striving |
| ☐ Competition | ☐ Criticism | ☐ Judgmental |
| ☐ Hypercritical | ☐ Cynical | ☐ Possessiveness |
| ☐ Covetousness | ☐ Isolation | ☐ Pride |
| ☐ Hyper Sexuality | ☐ Compulsive Lying | ☐ Lust |
| ☐ Self-Pity | ☐ Inferiority | ☐ Fear |
| ☐ Distrust | ☐ Disrespect | ☐ Perversion |
| ☐ Intolerance | ☐ Shame | ☐ Impatience |
| ☐ Vanity | ☐ Beastiality | ☐ Self Harm |
| ☐ Overly Apologetic | ☐ Control | ☐ Fear of Love |

# True Assesment

If you can identify with one of these items then you have experienced **rejection** and **abandonment**. If you struggle with a few or more then it is likely that you have endured a **trauma** due to **rejection** and **abandonment**. Now that we recognize that this is an area that everyone is affected. It's important to know that Jesus experienced this too. We love to glamorize His story for the children's books but His story was a story of constant **rejection** and **abandonment**. From sleeping in a manger at an early age, to the Pharisees constantly trying to publicly humiliate Him, even to His own Father turning His back on Him while hanging on the cross. We need to be confident in His story because that means that there are tools to remove the Rejection Complex and live in freedom.

**"So then, since Christ suffered physical pain, you must arm yourselves with the same attitude he had, and be ready to suffer, too. For if you have suffered physically for Christ, you have finished with sin." 1 Peter 4:1 NLT**

**"For God called you to do good, even if it means suffering, just as Christ suffered for you. He is your example, and you must follow in his steps." 1 Peter 2:21 NLT**

In today's exercise, create a timeline. Try to estimate the years that you remember struggling with the symptoms on your list. Then see if there are connections to a moment of rejection or abandonment around that time. This may take more than one try so be patient with yourself.

# Journal Moment

# Healing at the Source

Today let's explore **coping mechanisms**. Those are the things that you do to bring comfort whenever you feel **triggered**. So let's start with **triggers**.

Wikipedia defines a **trauma trigger** as a psychological stimulus that prompts involuntary recall of a previous traumatic experience. The stimulus itself need not be frightening or traumatic and may be only indirectly or superficially **reminiscent** of an earlier traumatic incident, such as a scent or a piece of clothing.

To elaborate, I feel most unsafe at night alone because this is the time of day that the abuse took place. **Triggers** could be music, smells, time, locations, conversations, ect. There are endless ways for your brain to categorize **trauma**.

Now that we recognize **triggers** we can identify how we **cope** with them. More obviously, substance abuse, hyper sexuality and mood adjustment. More subtle responses are shutting down, overspending, obsessive cleaning, and perfectionism. It's important to know that none of these are healthy or beneficial to your **healing** process.

Some **coping** mechanisms are beneficial, and taught by therapists. Some will even help you to advance your career. Some will help you to be better in the moment and to process your emotions. The only thing about coping is, you're just **coping**. It's all a temporary tool and it only will hold you until the next time that you need it. Our true goal is healing. I'll say it again for the people in the back, **HEALING**.

# Healing at the Source

"Now they came to Jericho. As He went out of Jericho with His disciples and a great multitude, blind Bartimaeus, the son of Timaeus, sat by the road begging. And when he heard that it was Jesus of Nazareth, he began to cry out and say, "Jesus, Son of David, have mercy on me!" Then many warned him to be quiet; but he cried out all the more, "Son of David, have mercy on me!" So Jesus stood still and commanded him to be called. Then they called the blind man, saying to him, "Be of good cheer. Rise, He is calling you." And throwing aside his garment, he rose and came to Jesus. So Jesus answered and said to him, "What do you want Me to do for you?" The blind man said to Him, "Rabboni, that I may receive my sight." Then Jesus said to him, "Go your way; your faith has made you well." And immediately he received his sight and followed Jesus on the road." Mark 10:46-52 NKJV

**Healing** MUST come from **faith**. Now in order for you to have **faith**, you have to know in whom you have **faith**. Also, you have to know what **faith** is.

"Now faith is the substance of things hoped for, the evidence of things not seen."
Hebrews 11:1 NKJV

I have to be frank, this is not a self help book and I don't believe that you can help yourself. This book is for those of us that believe in **Jesus Christ**. We believe that He is the son of God and an equal part of the triune Godhead; Father, Son, & Holy Spirit. He is the way, the truth and the life! No one can come to the Father except through Him. If you believe this (or want to), this book is for you.

Today: Let's dive into hope. Take a moment to speak with Jesus, honestly. Tell him why you are reading this book. Tell Him what you want to be healed from. Let's believe again that healing is possible. Then sit for a moment and some of you are ready to hear from Him. He may say something, if you don't hear anything, no worries, He definitely heard you.

# Journal Moment

# Arrested Development

Today is all about **childhood trauma**. Statistics show that the average child has decided what type of person they will be by age 11. If that is the case then, most of your life choices are determined by your individual human experience between ages 5 and 11. Not to say that a traumatic event can not happen after that point, but it is way more likely that it would take a major life event to change the trajectory of your thought process. So then what happens when **trauma** like grief, abuse, coercion, secrets, poverty, **abandonment**, excessive wealth, ect. occurs? These things become weights tied to you and your mental or emotional development. I tell people that I was emotionally 16 years old until I was 31. Every decision that I made was for that 16yr old sad girl that desperately wanted joy. I wore a happy face mask everyday while bleeding out emotionally.

**This is one of my journal entries from therapy:**
People think that I'm getting better but the truth is I'm not. I'm scared. All of the time not knowing where I am safe. Always looking over my shoulder. Tonight's dream was the worst. I dreamt that after catching a ton of the employees having sex. I was being raped by someone who obviously had herpes on his genitals. He also was one of the people having sex but with another man. In this dream I asked for help but none heard me. Eventually someone did and they stopped it but an old lady told me to sue and get my money. As if that would make me feel less disgusted.

Part of playing the "**I'm fine**" role is dealing with the **guilt** and **loneliness** of **lying** to all of your loved ones. Understanding and recognizing that you are living for the broken parts of you is the first step to changing your perspective and growing in a healthy way. So how do we move forward? Knowing the truth. The key to unlocking new growth is in a personal relationship with
**Jesus Christ**.

# Arrested Development

"Jesus said to the people who believed in him, "You are truly my disciples if you remain faithful to my teachings. And you will know the truth, and the truth will set you free." "But we are descendants of Abraham," they said. "We have never been slaves to anyone. What do you mean, 'You will be set free'?" Jesus replied, "I tell you the truth, everyone who sins is a slave of sin. A slave is not a permanent member of the family, but a son is part of the family forever. So if the Son sets you free, you are truly free." John 8:31-36 NLT

I know that it seems unlikely but stay with me. I will show you how I secured my victory through Him. Today I want you to assess where your relationship with Jesus is. Do you have one? Do you trust Him? Is HE Lord of your life? After you have made that assessment, I encourage you to dedicate this time of **healing** to Him. Let him know that after this you intend to share in true life with Him.

## Because of Jesus I am...

```
H F V H D E V O L N D N E D
G E C C D I N D D E D E S G
D P E E C E R O L E F D C V
C R E E C H T L T E L R R N
D O V O T H A R E A R A E A
F T I Y H C I C O T L L E E
D E T L D C E L O F S O C H
H C A O L E R E D A N E N D
D T E H H N M A V O     M E
H E R C L A E E F D F E C H
G D C E C I D S E T A G H A
U O F L T A V D O D E F O O
A D E A S L A E O H E D D D
L E E F F F S A F E C R O O
```

CALLED
HOLY
SAVED
CHILD OF GOD
LIVE
CHOSEN
HEALED
LAUGH
PROTECTED
CREATIVE
LOVED
SAFE
REDEEMED
CONFORTED
CRAFTED
FREE
NOT ALONE

# Journal Moment

# The Child Within

**READ: Genesis 37:3-35 NLT**

No one knows what familial **trauma** looks like more than Joseph. He was born with such a bright future and was literally thrown into a pit by his brothers for it. Today I'm speaking about **childhood trauma**. I was molested and abused at such a young age that love was not going to be a concept that I easily understood. Remember that there are key developmental factors during childhood and if certain boundaries are not taught or are broken, your brain receives the information as new facts and writes over the old facts.

Let's dive into my example.
**Fact:** My parents love me, I am safe with them.
**Abuse:** I have to keep this secret. My parents cannot love me like this. On the other hand they didn't protect me from this. They are not safe.

The new narrative was not true but it was my brain's best effort to make sense of my situation. But this rationalization hurt me immensely in the years to come. Secrets create lies, distrust creates rebellion, feeling unprotected creates an orphan complex.

By age 8 I had already been broken in love and made drastic attempts to find a cure. I knew of God's love but I didn't understand it and I considered it limited at best. I'm here to tell you that just because you don't understand something doesn't mean that it's not real or it is broken. God's love is **limitless** and He intends to give purpose to every **trauma** that you have endured! Let's take some time and identify some **Fake Facts** that you may have been living by. Let's look for supporting details that make them invalid.

Create new facts that support the evidence and read them out loud to yourself.

Ex. My parents made some poor choices that caused me pain but God can use my pain.

# Journal Moment

# Which Brother are You?

**READ: Genesis 37:3-35 NLT**

I know what you are thinking, she got lazy and used the same scripture twice. Well not this time. Today I wanted to look at the other **broken** children in this story. Joseph's brothers we so **rejected** that people even ignore their pain when they preach this passage. A lot of times children that were born when a parent has matured get a different version of a parent because they have grown in areas that they were still immature in when they were raising the older children. The first scripture of this passage states that Joseph's father loved him the most. When I read this I had to acknowledge his brother's **rejection**. As a middle child I can identify with feeling like my parents liked others more than me. Especially with some of the Fake Facts that my brain had accepted. Let's define something for a moment. **Jealousy** is a result of feeling less than for lacking something. Jealousy comes from a place of insecurity; insecurity comes from **rejection** and **abandonment**.

This type of **rejection** is **sibling rejection.** It's hardest to overcome because your siblings/ cousins should be your first set of friends. The constant comparison causes you to measure yourself to them instead of God. This is idolatry and covetousness and it is a never ending cycle if you don't surrender it to Jesus.

Example:
I never noticed my body was round until I got teased about it. Then, I noticed other's had a better shape then me. (Rejection)

By no means am I condoning selling Joseph into slavery. They allowed their **Fake Facts** to cause them to do a terrible thing. What my intent is to help you see how they struggled with **rejection** and **abandonment** before causing Joseph to go through the same thing. This is important because that's what broken people do. They break other people. **Healed** people heal people.

So are you Joseph or are you his brothers? In some cases you may be both. Identify a time that you may have hurt others while blinded by **Fake Facts**. Ask God to forgive you and forgive yourself. This may be a good time to ask them to forgive you as well.

# Journal Moment

Journal Moment

# Your Good, His Glory

I have taken a few flights in my life but there was one pivotal flight in my life. I was in the middle of my healing process and my cousins and I planned a cousin's trip. I sat by the window to not encourage anyone to speak to me. As I looked out of the window I noticed the ground and what it looked like as we were taking off. The further we ascended the smaller everything looked. At that moment God spoke to me and said, "See the bigger plan. It's not about you at all, but you are a big part of an even bigger plan." This moment was well before my transformation took place and I noticed that I experienced moments like this throughout my life. Moments of clarity and reminders that my identity was not attached to my situation.

**"You intended to harm me, but God intended it all for good. He brought me to this position so I could save the lives of many people." Genesis 50:20 NLT**

I want you to read this part aloud five times :
**Today is a new day. God is extending me a fresh portion of mercy. Everything in my past, God is going to turn around in my favor. When he does, I will proclaim his goodness, mercy, and faithfulness!**

When the brain hears something five times it registers it as a **fact**. Take a quick inventory of how you felt the first time that you said it versus the fifth time. Retraining your brain or "renewing your mind" is **your responsibility**.

Okay so let's get real for a moment. When someone used to tell me that God was turning it
around for my good, I used to get so annoyed. How could God allow rape in my life? How is that or my good? How does that bring Him any glory? Quite simply the response is **FOR HIS NAMESAKE**. We cannot truly know the sacrifice of Jesus without sharing in His pain. Without discovering what it means to endure. Had I not gone through molestation, lies, intimidation, rape, physical **abuse**, emotional **abuse**, **rejection**, **abandonment**, and so much more, there would be no book. I would not know Jesus on this personal level and I would not have a heart for His people.

# Your Good, His Glory

The truth is we have to get out of the mindset of "if I'm uncomfortable in life, this is a bad thing" most athletes know that you have not even started training until the pain comes. And even after the pain and numbness set in you keep going. You will never know how strong you are until you reach your breaking point and keep going. So today's admonishment is KEEP GOING **FOR HIS NAMESAKE**!

**"For whoever desires to save his life will lose it, but whoever loses his life for My sake will save it." Luke 9:24 NKJV**

**"Therefore do not be ashamed of the testimony of our Lord, nor of me His prisoner, but share with me in the sufferings for the gospel according to the power of God," II Tim 1:8 NKJV**

As we wind down today, take a moment to write down the worst moment you can think of and ask yourself and God how can He use it?

# Journal Moment

# When there is No Justice

As a child, I honestly did not know that I was molested. I believed what I was told and that I was a willing participant in sexual acts and that it was mutually beneficial. I was convinced that telling my story would not get me justice and I would get in trouble. By the time that I started intensive therapy, the statute of limitations had passed on one of the people that took advantage of me and the other was in prison for other crimes. I was convinced that I was over it and that moving on was the best thing for me. Only until it happened again. I was at a club after hours and the rapist was a club security guard. Some believe that I was drunk, I believe that I was drugged. I can still remember what it felt like to be bent over the dirty bathroom porcelain sink and him sarcastically saying that we have to do this again sometime as he returned my phone to me and sent me on my way.

I tried to do everything the right way but I found out very quickly that I wasn't going to get justice. The one camera in the area that would have shown him forcing himself into the bathroom behind me was "not working" at the time. The investigator showed me a book of laws that indicated my being under the influence by my own doing meant that I was able to give consent. I began to spiral with questions. How could this be? God, where is your justice? God, what are you going to do about this? People that I trusted were saying things like why were you even at the club? I wish that I knew then, what I know now. (READ: **Proverbs 28:5 NKJV**)

> **"For if we sin willfully after we have received the knowledge of the truth, there no longer remains a sacrifice for sins, but a certain fearful expectation of judgment, and fiery indignation which will devour the adversaries. Anyone who has rejected Moses' law dies without mercy on the testimony of two or three witnesses. Of how much worse punishment, do you suppose, will he be thought worthy who has trampled the Son of God underfoot, counted the blood of the covenant by which he was sanctified a common thing, and insulted the Spirit of grace? For we know Him who said, "Vengeance is Mine, I will repay," says the Lord. And again, "The Lord will judge His people." It is a fearful thing to fall into the hands of the living God." Hebrews 10:30 NKJV**

The seeds that we sow, grow in many different ways. God rewards how He wants AND when He wants, but it will always be a **just** reward. Well, so do His judgments. We may not see His judgment playing out on this side of Heaven but it will come. I must point out that it is truly arrogant to assume that you know a better punishment than God. Rather than looking for justice, let's take today to pray for the soul of those that have wronged you. **Forgiveness** is the way to **healing**.

# Journal Moment

# Hypothetical Loved Ones

We cannot talk about **rejection** or **abandonment** without discussing "who **abandoned** you". or some, this may be one person and for others, this may be a host of people. Today we will discuss both and how to heal relationships that are still struggling with this.

> "Jonathan son of Saul had a son who was lame in both feet. He was five years old when the news about Saul and Jonathan came from Jezreel. His nurse picked him up and fled, but as she hurried to leave, he fell and became disabled. His name was Mephibosheth." II Sam 4:4 NIV

Let's deal with child **abuse**. If you endured any **abuse** as a child or even witnessed **abuse** of any kind as a child, there were likely people that were supposed to protect you. No matter whom it was there is a distrust that possibly has been brewing between you since the incident or season of **abuse**. I want first and foremost to say that this is normal. However, is probably the most detrimental effect of childhood **trauma** and is definitely affecting your current relationships. I want to say this. Learning who to trust is important to the development of a child. We are going to spend a few sessions working on this child inside of you. Take some time to jot down a moment when you were **dropped**. Maybe it could be bullying or neglect or even overworked as a child. Then I want you to write down the person that was supposed to protect you. Next I want you to write this statement.

**(Insert Name)**, when I was a child **(Insert Event)** happened I was placed in your care and was left unprotected. In that moment I felt **(Insert Emotion)**. Today, that child renounces that emotion and releases you from all responsibility. Today I forgive you for not being able to protect me.
Now say it five times so it becomes a **fact**.

# Journal Moment

# Hypothetical Loved Ones II

Everyone wants to be **loved**, **needed**, and **accepted**. What happens when you don't feel that from family, church members, teammates, classmates, ect? There are two major responses:

**1. It's obviously me.**

Now let's preference this first response with: it is possible to make yourself challenging to love. We all have different responses to **rejection** and some people put up protective barriers around themselves to ensure that they **reject** others before enduring **rejection** themselves. But now that we have explored that response mechanism, we can really debunk this statement.

**You Are Lovable Because Christ Loved You First.**

*"But God clearly shows and proves His own love for us, by the fact that while we were still sinners, Christ died for us." Romans 5:8 AMP*

I cannot stress enough that this is NOT a "self help" book. We are working together to **heal your heart**. And the only one who can do this is **Jesus Christ**. So this scripture is one that we need to memorize and hide in your heart. The thought of being unlovable or undeserving of love is a lie from the enemy himself! And we reject that lie in the name of Jesus!

**2. They have a problem.**

I want to give you some scenarios:
There is a boy with no active father. Emotionally **orphaned**, raised by the streets because his mother is forced to work to support all of the children. This boy was made me feel less than at school because of this situation.

There is a town controlled by racism and the quality of a human being is determined by what side of town that a child lived and what school that they were afforded to attend. Even if this child left and became a skilled worker and worked their way into the other side of town, they were still **rejected** by them.

# Hypothetical Loved Ones II

There is a girl, **sexually abused** by her own drug addicted father and still forced to keep up with chores, make good grades, and raise other siblings. These are real stories and I know what you're thinking. What does that have to do with me? Understanding that **everyone has a story** helps you to understand that the people that were so called supposed to love and protect you may have done the best they could with what they had. I want you to read a birthday speech that I wrote for my dad. At this point of my life I was in therapy and was doing this very work. In order to heal, I needed to understand my father and his story. I needed to see him as a man and not a father.

Dad,
I remember back when you were in the military, sitting on the couch at 43 deer way, waiting for you to come home from work. Mommy used to tell me that I could see you and then it was straight to bed. That was enough for me. Life went on and as distractions took my attention I started to look at you less and less.
I want you to know that things are different now. I realize that when I look at myself, I see you. Not just the quirky tendencies that drive this family crazy but I see your struggles, Insecurities, your humor, and ability to overcome any obstacles that come your way.
The difference now is when I look at you, I see that it wasn't who you were that centered me before bed. It was what you stood for. Strength, Security, and now I see that the way to find myself is to be all in with God. Tomorrow is 60 for you but I celebrate 31 years of you being the only man on this earth that loved me, 100% and didn't see me as a challenge to conquer but a reflection of yourself. I love now more than ever and I still see you Dad! Happy Birthday!

I wrote this speech in tears and I had so much clarity in that moment. Now it's your turn. This may take days depending upon how many people you need to do this for. Write a letter to the person that was supposed to protect you or accept you. Now tell their story. Find the humanity in them and tell them that you forgive them. This is important because you will need people to see your story to understand and forgive you.

"Be kind and helpful to one another, tender-hearted [compassionate, understanding], forgiving one another [readily and freely], just as God in Christ also forgave you."
**Ephesians 4:32 AMP**

# Journal Moment

**Journaling your healing journey will be one of the best things that you can do. It will allow you to get a good idea of your growth. Full disclosure, some of your journal entries are going to scare you. As long as you are honest with yourself and God, you are moving in the right direction. God does not require complete understanding, He honors the same things that we do; trust, obedience, communication, love, loyalty, and honesty. I'm going to share some of my journal entries and use them as examples. Warning: These are raw and unedited. I need you to see that I went through this and if I can make it out, you can too.**

# Deception of Hyper Sexuality

**Journal Entry: "I am currency. Surrounded by men but still so lonely. Nobody wants me."**

**Hyper sexuality** is the same illusion as any popularity contest. I used to think that it was this huge flex that I could have any man in any room. I even at some points would challenge myself by selecting one just to see if I could go home with them. The only flaw is that it's only for one night. **Hyper sexuality** is just as much of a drug as any other. The concept of devaluing yourself because you don't feel valued is destructive and a very temporal fix. It creates an unhealthy cycle and an insatiable desire to be seen.

I know what you're thinking, why do we do it? We do it because it is easier to believe the lie that that's all you have to give than to trust that what someone stole from you is only a small portion of what you have to give to the person that God has hand picked for you. Here is a bit of proof that you are only hurting yourself.

> **"Flee sexual immorality. Every sin that a man does is outside the body, but he who commits sexual immorality sins against his own body." I Corinthians 6:18 NKJV**

Today's exercise is to write down what you would be able to give someone if you could never have sex again. Then begin to remind yourself of who you are. Ask God to forgive you for giving away what is not for anyone but the one who finds true value in those other things first.

# Journal Moment

# Identity Crisis

**Journal Entry: "I identify as straight not because I exclusively like men but because it's easier not to tell anyone that I am attracted to genuine connections. I like men: I'm submissive to them. I like women: I'm aggressive with them. I watch shemale porn but I don't know why. I told my sister this last night that I could be pan sexual but she stopped the conversation. She was too disgusted. I don't know what I want or what my sexual orientation is and I'm 31. And I have no one to talk to now."**

Reminder: Everyone wants to be **loved**, **needed**, and **accepted**. I cannot talk about **rejection** and **abandonment** without speaking on sexual orientation and identity. They go hand in hand. We are all living this human experience and we were created for connection. God created us for relationships with Him and others. However, he defined what type of relationships that we should engage in clearly in His Word.

**"For You formed my inward parts; You covered me in my mother's womb. I will praise You, for I am fearfully and wonderfully made; Marvelous are Your works, And that my soul knows very well." Psalms 139:13-14 NKJV**

**Read: John.3.1-20NKJV**

Because of sin already being in the world when you got here, you were born with a list of things that you will struggle with internally. Some will struggle with greed, others fear, others same sex attraction, others lying. I could really go on for days and there is no one singular thing that you could defeat in order to get into heaven. This is why we needed Jesus to die on the cross. The threat for **rejection** and **abandonment** is **loss of identity**.

Today, write a letter to yourself stating what makes you, you. Why? Do you like you? How do you know who you are?

# Journal Moment

# The Emotion that's Not from God

**Journal Entry:** "Last night i had a dream that I was in my childhood home and my abuser from then climbed through the window. I kept telling him that he doesn't belong here. All of the teenagers that lived in the house were arguing with me. Saying that I should calm down but I started whipping him with a belt until he climbed out but he stayed on the deck. I woke up."

**Journal Entry:** "I'm sad for myself, I'm afraid all of the time. I'm fine. I'm being dramatic. I have a problem."

When the boogie monster becomes real it's easy to get used to being afraid. At this point in my life, I was diagnosed with severe PTSD (**Post Traumatic Stress Disorder**). My brain was in a **trauma** state majority of the time and I was in intensive therapy and working all of my tools but I needed Jesus. I was so angry with Him that I had no clue that He was the key to my relief. This is the point that I must give you today. Without Jesus, fear is your fate.

**"For God has not given us a spirit of fear, but of power and of love and of a sound mind." II Timothy 1:7 NKJV**

Today was quick but not easy. In fact, this may take a few days. Ask God to help you to believe that He is the key to your safety. Ask Him to believe that there are better days ahead. Ask Him to help you to forget what you were afraid of.

# Journal Moment

# They Did Not Earn You

**Journal Entry:** "I had an old sex partner that was supposed to be my friend. He gave me get BV every time that we slept together. He told me last night that I was being nosey for responding to his social media when he seemed like he was going through something. He's been asking me to meet him at his house but I won't go. And this was my response: The truth is I care but I have no advice to give. I'm a mess right now. You are so selfish. You don't want to respect my boundaries. You hurt me deeply and I don't want to go to your house anymore. You made me feel wanted and rejected in the same bed. I'm afraid all of the time and no one checks up on me. They see me smile and think I'm good. But the only thing I'm good at is faking it because I've had to do it my whole life. (Maybe that's progress)"

**Journal Entry:** "I'm laying here I'm this bed wondering why I'm not good enough for him. He holds me like he knows what I need but doesn't want to give it to me and all I want to do is give me to him. But tonight will just be a memory to him. Yet for me it would mean starting over emotionally. How did I get here. Half naked with this man that my feelings have never really went away. And still in this moment, if he kissed me I would melt and submit to every thing that he wants to do. What's wrong with me?"

The toughest thing about giving yourself to people without them earning it is they take as much as you have and only give as much as they want. I used to be a professional friend with benefits without the benefit. I should have worn a banner that said "Use Me". I've bought jewelry, food, paid bills, opened up credit cards, had doctors appointments, and almost had children for individuals that never took me on a date. Why? I was convinced that as long as I was useful, people would value me. For the most part, it worked until I needed something in return. When I figured this out, I started taking advantage of other people that felt the same way that I once felt. I want to make this clear that anyone that truly values you will commit to you. I'm by now that you heard the popular TIKTOK phrase, "If they wanted to, they would." Marriage is the goal. Abiding in Jesus is the way!

# They Did Not Earn You

*"If you abide in Me, and My words abide in you, you will ask what you desire, and it shall be done for you."* John 15:7 NKJV

**My brokenness created a cycle**. I wasn't in need of a new partner or a boyfriend. I needed a relationship with **Jesus Christ**.

The same method of people pleasing that I had adapted to romantic relationships, translated to friendships and even familial relationships. **Rejection** and **abandonment** goggles have a way of making you feel that you are doing things for the right reasons. You may think that it's unkind to say no or that you are the only one that can be there for them. The truth is, people pleasing is one of the most selfish; self destructive things that one can do. The Oxford dictionary defines **motive** as a reason for doing something, especially one that is hidden or not obvious. Motives are subjective to the googles that you are looking through. The best way to clearly understand if you are doing something with pure motives is to not receive the love, admiration, recognition, and/or gratitude that your actions warranted (or so you thought). If we are doing things with this exchange in mind then we are using people as much as they are using you. We need to treat people as we want to be treated but expect to be treated like Jesus was treated.

Today, have a moment with yourself and God. Are you trying to skip ahead to a healthy relationship? Are you seeking approval in others instead of Christ? Are you ready to try abiding in Him?

# Journal Moment

# No More Self Harm

Oxford Dictionary defines "Self Harm" as deliberate injury to oneself, typically as a manifestation of a mental condition. Spiritually, self harm includes; drug and alcohol abuse, sexual sins, self sabotage, unforgiveness and more. As those are very real self harm tactics, today's focus is the more literal definition. We need to address the topic of suicide and self inflicted injury. My old self was guilty of suicidal ideation and suicide attempts. I can admit though, I never truly wanted to die, let alone die at my own hands. I felt more as if I just didn't want to live the way that I was living. I felt hopeless, helpless, and alone. I felt like there were no other options.

We could spend hours thinking about why we self harm but it would be useless. The truth is whatever we fix our eyes on, we will see. If we look to Jesus, we will see our true way of escape. We did not create ourselves. We did not die for ourselves. We do not get to hurt ourselves.

**"The temptations in your life are no different from what others experience. And God is faithful. He will not allow the temptation to be more than you can stand. When you are tempted, he will show you a way out so that you can endure." 1 Corinthians 10:13 NLT**

Learn from Job. We who believe, have everything that we need to make it through any situation. See God does give you more than you can bear. Because it helps us to remember that in Him we live, move, and have our being!

**""If only you would prepare your heart and lift up your hands to him in prayer! Get rid of your sins, and leave all iniquity behind you. Then your face will brighten with innocence. You will be strong and free of fear. You will forget your misery; it will be like water flowing away. Your life will be brighter than the noonday. Even darkness will be as bright as morning. Having hope will give you courage. You will be protected and will rest in safety. You will lie down unafraid, and many will look to you for help. But the wicked will be blinded. They will have no escape. Their only hope is death."" Job 11:13-20 NLT**

Today's exercise is simple but it take guts. I challenge you to write down what you really think that you cannot escape. This week or even month, make this your focus of prayer. But this time, Pray in confidence that God will deliver you. Also, if ever you need to speak with someone. Just call **988**, the **Suicide and Crisis Lifeline**, available 24hrs a day.

# Journal Moment

# Abandonment through Loss

It may be easy to assume that saying "goodbye" to a loved one is simple, but if we dive deep into the complex emotions concerning grief, we would easily find that **abandonment** may cause anger and frustration. You may have thoughts like I should've been the one who died in or Why did you have to leave so soon? Or even in the loss of a parent it could be why did you leave before I was ready? Reality is it's OK to say, I feel **abandoned** by someone else passing. In fact, simply acknowledging that fact, could be the most freeing part of your recovery today, whether it be a tragic accident or a school shooting or even death of natural causes, we develop a relationship with individuals and have an unrealistic perspective. That time is a commodity for him and we say things like I'll call you tomorrow and we even make plans to visit months ahead.

In all actuality the only thing guaranteed is that we are not guaranteed the promise of tomorrow so in understanding and dissecting the issue of **abandonment** through loss. We have to understand the purpose and the care that we have towards each other. There's a famous old statement that says "do what you can while you can. ". It's just that simple, that is our purpose towards each other to do what we can for each other while we are allotted time on this planet. Now yes, a mother has a responsibility to raise a child however, dad's plan is bigger and more complex than that. In some instances, a mothers only job was to bring a child into this world, and in other instances, a mothers only job was to teach them the basics. We can not truly understand what and why God allows but we know one thing, we can ask him the right questions.

1. Help me to see your hand in this.
2. What do you want me to keep from this experience?
3. How can you get the glory?
4. Who needs to hear this?

We have to understand that true relationship with the Father through His Son Jesus means that we recognize that everything in our life was known since before time began.

> "For You formed my inward parts; You covered me in my mother's womb."
> Psalms 139:13 NKJV

Today and this week, let's ask God the right questions and be still and wait for Him to answer.

# Journal Moment

# Healing your Support System

> "Listen carefully: Unless a grain of wheat is buried in the ground, dead to the world, it is never any more than a grain of wheat. But if it is buried, it sprouts and reproduces itself many times over. In the same way, anyone who holds on to life just as it is destroys that life. But if you let it go, reckless in your love, you'll have it forever, real and eternal."
> John 12:24-25 MSG

Today I'm really excited to discuss your progress and reflect on how God has elevated your thinking. So depending on your level of distress, you may have a circle of people that are helping you and maybe even praying for you. Some may call them your support system. At this point they have held you up while you were bleeding out in **trauma**. It's hard to grasp but they have taken part in your experience.

For me it was my family and church family. They watched me spiral from an 8 year terrible marriage in combination with all of my unresolved **trauma**. I was on suicide watch twice but had experienced suicidal ideation many times. They saw the joy that I'd once exuded disappear. There is one fact that I want to drive home. **This was traumatic for them**. It's important to recognize that you were the grain of wheat that had to die to become who you are today. This was scary for your loved ones. When you go through something, the people that love you go through as well. If you go to prison, they do too. This was a difficult concept for me because I felt very alone in my pain. But you will never heal the support system until you acknowledge their trauma. Now I'm not saying that it's your fault, I'm saying that **their experience was real**.

As you heal, it may look ugly first. Here are some signs that your support system needs **healing**.
- They don't believe that the healing inside of you is real and permanent.
- They have gotten so used to caring for you that they almost don't want you to get better.
- They are hovering or won't give you independence.

Let's pray for them today.

Father God,
I thank you for the people that you strategically placed in my life to support me through my toughest seasons. I pray that you bless them indeed! I also ask you to heal their hearts and minds toward the trauma that they went through while caring for me.

In the name of Jesus, Amen.

# Journal Moment

# The Prison of Procrastination

By now I have been laboring with this book for over a year, almost two years. My journey of **rejection** and **abandonment** has had many victories as well as challenges. But the biggest obstacle that I have had to face is **procrastination**. The enemy, our one adversary, has a very small bag of tools that will surely derail your healing and purpose. Procrastination will be one of your biggest obstacles. Whether you are at the beginning of this journey or well into your healing process, if you can be distracted, you can be stopped. As you continue your journey of healing and relationship with God, overcome distractions and procrastinating by this one acronym **S.T.A.R.T.**

**S- Stay focused on you mission or goal**

**T- Turn away from distractions**

**A- Alter your habits to make room for healing.**

**R- Remove ANYTHING (anyone) that takes the place of God in your life.**

**T- Take time away from one thing and replace it with the Word of God.**

**"Now it happened as they journeyed on the road, that someone said to Him, "Lord, I will follow You wherever You go." And Jesus said to him, "Foxes have holes and birds of the air have nests, but the Son of Man has nowhere to lay His head." Then He said to another, "Follow Me." But he said, "Lord, let me first go and bury my father." Jesus said to him, "Let the dead bury their own dead, but you go and preach the kingdom of God." And another also said, "Lord, I will follow You, but let me first go and bid them farewell who are at my house." But Jesus said to him, "No one, having put his hand to the plow, and looking back, is fit for the kingdom of God."" Luke 9:57-62**

# Journal Moment

# Fearing What You Desire

*"Such love has no fear, because perfect love expels all fear. If we are afraid, it is for fear of punishment, and this shows that we have not fully experienced his perfect love."*
**1 John 4:18 NLT**

As we wrap up this phase of your **healing**, I want to warn you about the **fear of love**. This is one of the most sneaky symptoms of **rejection** and **abandonment**. We tend to use it as a shield or protective barrier from re-injuring ourselves. It causes us to withdraw, question others motive, and isolate ourselves.

I recently had a knee injury that caused me to be hospitalized. Prior to this injury, I had been fearlessly climbing trees, jumping in and out of a pickup truck and doing anything that one would think that a 4ft 9in woman cannot do. Now that I am in recovery, I am way more cautious about how I treat that knee. I have created a new list of limitations and even favor it from time to time.

This is what we tend to do in **love**. By now your walk with Jesus is strengthening. Please be aware that He is going to allow you to be put in situations that are going to test your **trust** in Him. To this I say, don't limit yourself. Love is vulnerable, and to someone that has been hurt, it may feel scary. But it is also, one of the greatest things that we were created for!

**READ: 1 Cor 13 NKJV**

- **Love** unconditionally.
- **Love** without expecting a reward.
- **Love** those who curse you.
- **Lord** the Lord with your heart, soul, strength.
- **Love** what God loves.
- **Love** with trust that God has your back.

As the last prompt, write your **testimony**. This is where God turns everything that you have gone through into your greatest weapon. Sharing this, brings meaning to your obstacles while encouraging others through theirs. Remember: We overcome by the Blood of the Lamb and the Word of our **TESTIMONY**.

# Journal Moment

Made in the USA
Middletown, DE
18 November 2024